A Ten Years' Residence in France during the severest part of the Revolution; from ... 1787 to 1797, containing ... anecdotes of some of the most remarkable personages of that period.

Charlotte West

A Ten Years' Residence in France during the severest part of the Revolution; from ... 1787 to 1797, containing ... anecdotes of some of the most remarkable personages of that period.
West, Charlotte
British Library, Historical Print Editions
British Library
1821
8°.
791.h.14.

The BiblioLife Network

This project was made possible in part by the BiblioLife Network (BLN), a project aimed at addressing some of the huge challenges facing book preservationists around the world. The BLN includes libraries, library networks, archives, subject matter experts, online communities and library service providers. We believe every book ever published should be available as a high-quality print reproduction; printed on- demand anywhere in the world. This insures the ongoing accessibility of the content and helps generate sustainable revenue for the libraries and organizations that work to preserve these important materials.

The following book is in the "public domain" and represents an authentic reproduction of the text as printed by the original publisher. While we have attempted to accurately maintain the integrity of the original work, there are sometimes problems with the original book or micro-film from which the books were digitized. This can result in minor errors in reproduction. Possible imperfections include missing and blurred pages, poor pictures, markings and other reproduction issues beyond our control. Because this work is culturally important, we have made it available as part of our commitment to protecting, preserving, and promoting the world's literature.

GUIDE TO FOLD-OUTS, MAPS and OVERSIZED IMAGES

In an online database, page images do not need to conform to the size restrictions found in a printed book. When converting these images back into a printed bound book, the page sizes are standardized in ways that maintain the detail of the original. For large images, such as fold-out maps, the original page image is split into two or more pages.

Guidelines used to determine the split of oversize pages:

• Some images are split vertically; large images require vertical and horizontal splits.
• For horizontal splits, the content is split left to right.
• For vertical splits, the content is split from top to bottom.
• For both vertical and horizontal splits, the image is processed from top left to bottom right.

A

TEN YEARS'

RESIDENCE IN FRANCE,

&c. &c.

A

TEN YEARS' RESIDENCE

IN

FRANCE,

DURING THE

SEVEREST PART OF THE REVOLUTION;

FROM THE YEAR 1787 TO 1797,

CONTAINING

VARIOUS ANECDOTES

OF SOME OF THE

MOST REMARKABLE PERSONAGES OF THAT
PERIOD.

BY CHARLOTTE WEST.

London:

PRINTED FOR WILLIAM SAMS, NO. 1, ST. JAMES'S-STREET;
AND ROBERT JENNINGS, 2, POULTRY.

1821.

ADVERTISEMENT.

The following Work, if it may be allowed to deserve the name, is written under peculiar circumstances; and the occurrences of the times will, I hope, justify the publication of the facts contained therein.

I shall further state, in as concise a manner as possible, by way of Preface, that in the year

a

1787, my husband and self left England to reside in France, having no other motive or object in view (like many of the present day) than œconomy. After a few days of sunshine (comparatively speaking in the Book of Time) our horizon became overcast by the clouds of contention—and in the overwhelming flood of a Revolution we were swept away (into confinement and misery) with many of the unfortunate natives of the land we lived in; but years have passed away since then, and I have silently submitted to the will of Fate; but when my native land is threatened (as has been lately the case) with all the horrors of a Revolution, shall I sit supinely without adding my mite for its protection, by setting forth the dreadful events I have been an eye-witness of, and a bodily sufferer under the rigorous measures of a Revolutionary Government. No! forbid it all the powers of memory, and love to my country, in whose cause every nerve feels doubly strung in her defence. But, alas! my strength, what avails it! all that I have in my power is to shew the fallacy of running riot after a phantom, like the dog in the fable, who let go the substance for the shadow. My best wishes shall ever be while I live, for England, her King, and Constitution.

Now these her Princes are come home again,
Come, the three corners of the world in arms,
And we shall shock them: nought shall make us rue,
If England to herself do rest but true.

Begging the Public's kind indulgence,
For this my first,
(And in all probability my last)
Essay.
I have the honour to remain,
Their most obedient and
Very humble servant,

THE AUTHOR.

21 OC 62

NAMES OF SUBSCRIBERS.

———

Bennet, ———, esq. one copy.

Brown, Mrs. one copy.

Burrowes, A. D. esq. one copy.

Bosquet, Francois D. esq. one copy.

Cluer, Edward William, esq. one copy.

Chapman, Captain, three copies.

Cuff, Mrs. one copy.

Cooke, Miss Jane, one copy.

Doyle, Major-General Sir Charles, one copy.

Doyle, Lady, one copy.

Dewes, Captain John, late Paymaster 28th
        Foot, one copy.

Dewes, Mrs. one copy.

Dewes, James, esq. one copy.

Dewes, William, esq. one copy.

Ferrand, Robert, esq. M.P. one copy

Fletcher,   esq. one copy.

Foot,   esq. one copy.

Fellowes, Mrs. two copies.

Fellowes, Miss, two copies.

Fermer, Mrs. two copies.

Glenville,   esq. one copies.

Griffiths, Mrs. one copy.

Gibson, Mrs. Joseph, one copy.

————, ————, esq. six copies.

Hoare, Hugh H. esq. three copies.

Hill, Thomas, esq. two copies.

Harper, Edward, esq. one copy.

Harper, esq. one copy.

Hayward, James William, esq. one copy.

Ingle, Mrs. one copy.

Ingle, Henry, esq. one copy.

Johnston, Doctor John, of Armagh, Ireland,
      one copy.

Irby, Miss, one copy.

Jerningham, Mrs. one copy.

Lethbridge, Sir Thomas, M.P. one copy.

Lethbridge, Lady, one copy.

Lethbridge, Rev. Charles, three copies

Lloyd, Samuel, esq. one copy.

Lawrence, Benjamin, esq. one copy.

Morlidge, John, esq. one copys

Main, Miss, one copy.

Meoiller, Mrs. one copy.

Ongle, Lady, one copy.

Pettit, J. W. one copy.

Pattle, Mrs. one copy.

Quarrier, Mrs. one copy.

Ridge, Miss, one copy.

Randell, Reuben, esq. one copy.

Ramsbottom, John, esq. M.P. two copies.

Ramsbottom, Mrs. one copy.

Rowlands, Thomas Wood, esq. three copies.

Richards, Samuel, esq. one copy.

Spry, Rev. John, one copy.

Simes, Captain, one copy.

Simes, Miss, one copy.

Sanders, Thomas, esq. one copy.

Smith, Charles S. esq. one copy.

Suckling, Mrs. Colonel, one copy.

Treves, Mrs. Pelerine, six copies.

Timlin, esq. one copy.

Wyatt, Jeoffry, esq. one copy.

Wyatt, Philip, esq. one copy.

Wolrige, Lieutenant and Adjutant, Royal Marine Artillery, one copy.

Williams, Charles M. esq. one copy.

21 OC 62

CONTENTS.

——

CHAPTER I.

CHAPTER VI.

CHAPTER VII.

CHAPTER VIII.

CHAPTER IX.

CHAPTER X.

CHAPTER XI.

CHAPTER XII.

CHAPTER XIII.

CHAPTER XIV.

CHAPTER XV.

CHAPTER XVI.

CHAPTER XVII.

CHAPTER XVIII.

CHAPTER XIX.

A

TEN YEARS' RESIDENCE

IN

FRANCE.

CHAPTER I.

LEAVING ENGLAND—DESCRIPTION OF A VINTAGE IN
CHAMPAIGN.

In the year one thousand seven hundred and eighty-seven, my husband and self set off for France. Economy being the order of the day, we took up our abode in that delightful country La Champaigne, where we lived cheap and happy. In the winter we enjoyed an elegant and enlightened society. There was a *depôt* in that town of the garde de corps, and a number of them had their families residing there, which made it very pleasant.

The town of Cháillons is but small; it contained only ten thousand inhabitants at that time; and being a place of no business or manufactory (if I except the making of a few casks for wine) it seems a place well adapted for persons of small fortune to live at.

All the first necessaries of life are cheap and good; corn grows plentifully in the neighbourhood, and the vineyards are within twenty miles of the town. I longed for the next autumn to see and judge for myself. It came, and, being a fine season, fully answered, in reality, all those glowing encomiums which I had heard bestowed on a vintage in Champaign.

It is impossible for any one in this country to appreciate the beauty of a vintage who has never seen one. You are surrounded by hills, and the villages are seen as it were hanging on their sides, enclustered by the vines, whose mellow fruit are just ripe, and ripening for the use of man; the fine warm sun in the middle of the day, after a little sharp frost in the morning, makes all the villagers happy, as it portends a good vintage, *et de bon vin.*

The vintage lasts from five to six weeks altogether, and in that space of time must the vigneron collect his little all, which is to last him till that time comes round again. But it is a precarious property, and a man ought not to meddle with it, unless he has something else to depend on, for should there come a wet season (which is sometimes the case) a poor man is badly off indeed, because he is obliged to sell his wine at an improper season, to enable him to work the vines for the ensuing year. The rich man buys it up cheap, can afford to keep it by him, and sells it for more than double what it cost him.

I remember one very wet season, when they had so much wine that they had not casks enough to put it in, so much so, that any one who took two casks had one full one back with him, for the one he left behind, but it was hardly worth carrying away, as quality, not quantity, makes the poor man amends for all his labour.

CHAPTER II.

THE EX-EMPRESS JOSEPHINE.

I HAD a country-house in the beautiful village of Pierré, noted for its good wine, and the many gentlemen's estates and houses in it; the French compare it to a little Paris, for the company that resorted to it, and number of carriages that rolled through it (before the Revolution) at the time of the vintage.

And here let me speak of a personage whom I had the pleasure of meeting five days out of seven, during the vintage of 1788, who has since that time played a great character on the stage of Europe. I mean the empress Josephine; she was, at that time the countess de Beauharnois, on a visit at a gentleman's house with two of her daughters, * of about thirteen or fourteen years of age.

---

* One of them, some two or three years after, was married to Louis Buonaparte, and was afterwards queen of Holland.

Madame de Beauharnois was not remarkable for beauty, nor at that time youth, nor do I think she ever had been handsome ; but there was, as the Frénch express it, a *J'ne sais quoi* about her, which was irresistible. In her company you forgot youth, beauty, and every thing else, in the fascinating manners and wit, in the person of madame de Beauharnois. She had at that time two of her sons serving with their father, and who afterwards emigrated with him to the army of the prince de Condé.

If I had been asked what I thought her age was at that time, I should have said about forty-one or two. Poor soul! she was deserving of a better fate ; and thus much I must say, that let her conduct be what it would afterwards, she must have been drawn into it by unforeseen circumstances, for there was by no means any levity of conduct in her behaviour that warranted such a supposition ; and I hope from the number of lives that she certainly saved, and her extensive charities to the poor emigrants and others, that those sins will be forgiven that she was drawn into by the Revolution. She did not die a natural death ; who may have to answer for that in the next world, I must leave to him who knows all things.

I must not forget to relate the melancholy fate of one of my neighbours, in the same village of Pierré. A monsieur de la Motte, a most amiable man and far advanced in years, for he was then near eighty ; he had married late in life, and had a young family of two sons and one daughter ; the latter was under age, but the sons were two or three-and-twenty.

At the beginning of the Revolution, among the numbers who emigrated, they were of different descriptions; the first, the princes and the first nobility, under the idea of forming an army, and getting the foreign powers to join them to enter France with a formidable force, to reinstate their king, and restore that order which was lost, but they never reflected that while they were absent, they left their king in the tiger's gripe,

The next body that emigrated (for I shall class them under three heads) were those who emigrated for *fashion,* as those who were left behind, were thought *nobodys,* because *they* were not gone also:

The third class who emigrated were *literally nobodys,* and they thought by partaking of the fortunes of the princes and noblesse, that when they entered France again with an army that would reconquer and regenerate her, they should then *be somebodys.*

Of the *second* class were my two young friends, and in consequence of their emigration, all the property of the poor old father was confiscated, and himself sent to Paris, and there imprisoned; his dutiful and beautiful daughter attending him to the prison, where she remained till the day he was guillotined. I think, without exception, she was the most beautiful little person I ever saw in my life; but her *face*, whenever I looked at her, always brought to my mind Mrs. Fitzherbert, and what *she* must have been at the age of my young friend.

The day that her father was guillotined she mounted the scaffold with him, and entreated on her knees to spare her father's life, and take her's instead; she was frantic with despair; she laid her head under the fatal knife, and begged the executioner to sever her head from her body, or that if she could not save her father, at least she might die with him; but all would not do; they would not save her father's life, and her head was too beautiful to be cut off.

A gentleman who was present at the execution, was so struck with her filial piety and beauty, he thought that so much feeling and so· dutiful a daughter could not make a bad wife, and after due time had been given her to dry her tears, and let reason resume her sway, he offered her his hand and fortune.　They were married.

The father was upwards of eighty years of age when he was guillotined.

In the spring of 1790, we formed a party to go to Rheims, with an intention to see that famous city, not only for its being the capital of the province of Champaign, but also for its being the city, in which all the kings of France are consecrated on the coronation. All the gentlemen of our party were Freemasons, and knowing that my husband was one, they so arranged it, that we should be there on a lodge night, and of course *he* went with them.　In the same house were held two lodges, the one male and the other for female Maçonnes.　I was proposed, and in due time was initiated.　Be not alarmed, my fair country-women! but smile if you will—such things are not common in this country—nor you, my Brethren of Britain, frown not! though females are not allowed by English Masonry—yet, the

sister kingdom can boast of one *female mason
as good as any ;* and many there are in France
who do honour to the Craft: But *even* in that
country, they do not make women Masons, without great discrimination, as *every* woman is not
adapted by nature (through want of *nerve,* or
some other reason) to be a Freemason. Not one
of you, my Brethren, honour Masonry more than
I do; and remember a *certain Text in Scripture,*
&c. &c. &c. I had the pleasure of attending
the Lodge as often as the distance we lived at
would permit (thirty miles) for about two years
and a half, till the Dæmons of Discord crept in
among the people, (Masonry is not so common
in France among the labouring class as it is in
England) and they thought that the meetings of
the Freemasons were only held up as an excuse
for the Aristocrats to assemble to *plot* and ruin
the cause of the *bons patriots,* and we were
obliged to give it up.

NOTE—"The Author's best compliments to Mr. SAMS—
and as she has some doubt as to the propriety of inserting
the above, which treats on Masonry, she wishes for his
opinion on it before it goes to the Press—as she would be
extremely sorry to give any offence to that very respectable
Society."

The Publisher's Reply—

" Mr. SAMS presents his most respectful compliments to the Author, and begs to inform her, that HE has the honour of being a Freemason, and that he thinks no offence can possibly be given to the Craft by the insertion."

CHAPTER III.

THE ANNIVERSARY OF THE DESTRUCTION OF THE BASTILE.

CHALLONS sur Marne is about one hundred and sixty miles from Paris, (and the circulation of news is not so quick in that country as in this) and very little of what was passing there came to our knowledge till the destruction of the Bastile took place, at which we all heartily rejoiced, for the use that it was put to was a disgrace to a Christian country in the eighteenth century; and I think I might date the beginning of the Revolution from that day, at least it was so with us.

The affairs of France were beginning to look very gloomy, but we being strangers lived on, like a man who lives on a mountain, who sees the storm gathering beneath, and hears the crush of the little world below, without even supposing that it can reach him; so it was with us. Fatal security!

The 14th of July, 1791, was a gay day for Challons; every one was alert, the volunteers running in all directions; women and children dressed in their holiday clothes, all assembled on the promenade of the town. The morning service (or grand mass) was to be performed in the open air, with a canopy of celestial blue to cover us: sixty ladies had agreed to walk in procession on this grand occasion, and I made one of them; we were all dressed in white, decorated with garlands of flowers, intermixed with the tri-coloured ribbon, and a sash of the same hanging from the right shoulder to the left side; all the gentlemen of the town dressed in their uniforms and under arms; music playing, flags flying, drums beating, and all together made a very grand appearance.

I, who had been born in a country where every one loves his king, and respects the laws, felt no difficulty in holding up my right hand, and said *Je jure* (the oath proposed was to swear to defend the king and the laws) and every one held up his right hand and said *Je jure* (I swear) *de maintenir le roi et la loi.*

The ceremony and service being ended, we adjourned to dinner, and sat down more than five hundred persons. The king's riding-house had been prepared for the occasion, and the table was in the shape of an horse shoe; the sixty ladies sitting at the round end or top (no other females were admitted.) We went to dinner about three o'clock, and sat till the music called us to the merry dance a little after five, and we kept it up till past five the next morning; and thus began the first of the Revolution in that part of the country, with praying, feasting, and dancing; but we paid for it very shortly afterwards.

CHAPTER IV.

HUSSARDS DE LA MORT—AND DIGRESSION ON
REVOLUTIONS.

THE troops were marching in all directions, and many shocking cruelties had been committed in Paris and elsewhere, but our town of Challons was not long behind with them. One day arrived in great haste the old general Luckner (afterwards guillotined in Paris at upwards of eighty years of age.) He said he was come to put himself at the head of his army of 53,000 men, which he was told he should find in that town; but we had at that time only 10,000, and that was as many as inhabitants, and amongst that number we had three regiments of Hussards de la Mort, well known by the name of the Marsellois, but who were neither more or less than all the butcher boys and drovers of Paris regimented, and dressed in a hussard's dress of yellow and black cloth, with a death's head and two bones laid across under the head, in front of the cap and on the front of both arms, which had a most terrific appearance, the death's head and bones being black on a yellow ground; and that gave rise to the name which they had adopted.

These pretty boys, many of whom the " razor ne'er had graced their chins," nor had the oldest of them seen his twenty-third year, nor did they live to be much older, death claimed them for his own. Thanks to general Dumourier, as will be seen hereafter. These boys fancied that they were the voice of the great nation, embodied in their sweet persons, and that it was to rise or fall by their prowess, which they took care to exercise on all occasions, where they met with no resistance, or where they out-numbered their opponents; and this gallant conduct they carried on towards all well-dressed persons, male or female, calling them Aristocrates, or any thing else that came in their heads.

I was very near being the victim of one of them. One evening as I was going out to a party, I had on a black hat and feathers, with a black cockade in it, which gave one of these *gentlemen* offence, and he desired me instantly to take it out. I refused, and said that it was a part of my dress, and not put there for any other purpose. My husband was with me, whose arm

I pressed hard, and said in English, "For heaven's sake, don't speak; let me manage him." All this time we kept walking on, disputing as we went, and more than once he put his hand to his sabre, and half drew it; that took no effect on me. How to account for it I know not; but the more he insisted, the more resolute was I not to do it; and thus we went on till we arrived at the house I was going to, when he very quietly said to me, " Citizen, take my advice, and take that black cockade out of your hat; it is a mark of Aristocracy; you may meet with some of my comrades, who may not treat you quite so civilly as I have done. *Bon soir, bon soir.*"— And a good night thought I : I am glad you are gone; and now I'll take it out.

I told my friends of my adventure, who I am sure were more frightened for me than I had been for myself, and I got well scolded by my husband for my obstinacy as he called it.

Some few days after the above circumstance more troops arrived to the number of what the general expected. They were so thick in the town, that it was quite shocking; some of the inhabitants had thirty, some forty to lodge; and when in the town they were walking and lying about the streets like sheep in a field; they staid with us three days. All this body of men, some troops of the line, some volunteers, they did not agree well together, as they were jealous of each other, and the troops of the line hated the volunteers. Had they staid three days longer, I think we must have had a famine, if not a battle; nor were they satisfied with their general; he was very old, and added to that he was a foreigner; and they thought he intended to betray them, when he got them in front of the enemy. All that he could say, in very bad French, had no effect on them, when he said he would *doné son Tete a coupé*, if he betrayed them. Great disputes and confusion took place among them.

Some friends called on me, and asked me if I would take a walk to the Maison-de-Ville, to see what was going on; I agreed, and when we got there, there might be about two thousand persons present, military and others. The disputes ran very high about pay, clothing, &c. The troops brought two twelve pounders (irresistible arguments) to enforce their officers' demands. They had planted them immediately in front of the Maison-de-Ville with *lighted matches* over the touch-hole, ready to fire at a signal given; but I cannot say that I was much alarmed about it, for I looked at it only as a little gasconading, for I concluded that while their officers were there, that we were all safe enough.   But at length, if they did not get all they asked for, they got some, but it left them in a very ill humour, and they were determined some one should pay for it before the day closed; they selected two, a lieutenant-colonel of one of the regiments of the line, who had in some way or other, offended these *heroes* de la Mort; they took him down to the river side, and literally cut him to pieces.

The next victim of their rage and *valour* was, poor old Monsieur Chánláire, a king's counsellor. I knew him well; he was near ninety years of age, quite deaf and nearly blind.   He was walking with his female servant, who supported and took care of him, Nor his stoop of years, nor his feeble steps, nor all those could save him from their fell grasp.   He was met by a party of those valiant youths, who asked him if he was not an Aristocrat?   He being deaf, thought they asked if he was a *bon patriot* he said *(oui)* yes, when they instantly laid hold of him, and in the name of the *patri* and *la liberté*, cut off his nose, and most barbarously treated him, too shocking to relate, and they wantonly prolonged his misery for an hour and a half, before they gave him the *coup-de-grace,* before they killed him.

Oh! here let me pause! for the recollection of that horrid day still curdles the blood in my veins, even at this distance of time. And in this place let me apostrophise thee, Oh! Liberty, known by all, by name, but understood by few. How many, Oh, Goddess born! in thy name, commit the most unheard of cruelties, the newest kind of ways! No; it is thy frantic sister, Licentiousness, who profanes thy name, and fools and knaves lay hold on her, and call on thee. Now, what are thy attributes, Oh, Liberty! the love of social order; the giver of wholesome laws, which protect man from man, and defend the king upon his throne, and the cobler in his stall; and he that would dethrone his king, would rob the poor cobler also, could he gain any thing by it.

And now permit me to point out the mistaken notion of a Revolution bringing Liberty and Reform. It is a stalking-horse for all designing men, and in such mouths as theirs, leads the people from their quiet homes, to answer their *own ambitious* and *vile* purposes. I have seen it *nearly,* and felt it *severely,* and can

D

vouch for the truth. The French Revolution is
not so long gone by, but some must still remember that many who began the *change* were cut
off by greater rogues than themselves. The
duke of Orleans, who, at the head of all the
fish-women, water-carriers, and others, brought
Louis Seize and his family from Versailles to Paris,
and that monster of iniquity, Robespierre, and
many others, did not live to profit by the *havoc*
they had made; they were all guillotined: and
what is now the result! Why, after a struggle
of eight-and-twenty years—after deluging all
Europe with the blood of millions, the wheel
has gone round, and stands *just* where it *did*,
and ready to turn again by the first that shall
put his hand to it.

Oh! could my humble endeavours and advice
prevail on those who are *panting* for liberty, to
read these lines, and see in their mind's eye
what I have seen in reality; surely, they would
stop their headlong career, and spare the blood
of thousands; but should my poor country be
visited by such a calamity (which God of his infinite mercy forbid) I would advise the nobility,
and every man of property and probity, not to
abandon their king, as the French noblesse did,
when most he stood in need of their advice and

assistance. No; I would have them rally round the throne and the king, and by protecting him, they would protect their own property, themselves, and their families: at the worst it is better to be of king Richard's opinion, to *die* with harnness on one's *back*, rather than *tamely submit* to the *guillotine* or the *hangman*.

Ten thousand pardons for having trespassed on the patience of my kind readers; but did they know how my feelings are roused, when speaking or writing on the French Revolution, I am sure they would think and feel as I do.

A little while after, the murder of those two poor individuals in our town, general Lükenar was sent to Paris, and to prison, from which he was never released, till he was guillotined. General Dumourrier was made commander-in-chief of the army of the North, and we had the pleasure of getting rid of our very unwelcome guests. They were ordered to join the army, as there was a great battle expected to be fought very soon. They petitioned, or rather demanded, of their general, to have the post of honour in that day's fight, though there were yet many regiments of the line still left. Dumourrier promised them they *should;* and on the day that the famous battle of Jemappe was fought, they were put in front of the line, with *secret orders* to the *old regiments* that were placed behind, that if any *one* of the hussards gave *way, they* were to have *their* bayonets ; so that what with the *cannon* of the enemy, and the *bayonets* of their *friends,* there was not one of them left to say who had gained the day.

Dumourrier wrote to the Convention to say, that thirty thousand of the enemy (and I am sure at least as many of their own) had *bit* the *dust* in that *day's fight,* and that France had *only one man wounded,* and that was in his *little finger.* Mention honorable and *insertion* in *bulletin,* and Dumourrier had well *merited* of the *patrie.*

CHAPTER V.

THE ARREST OF THE KING OF FRANCE AND FAMILY AT VARENNES ON THE 20th JUNE, 1792.

Soon after we had got rid of our aforesaid troops we had a fresh arrival, but of a very different description; it was de Walshe's Irish brigade. The regiment had its halting-day. We had a captain Robertson sent to us to lodge, as every householder lodges a portion of troops individually in that country. We asked him to dine with us, and in the course of conversation, finding our sentiments corresponded with his own, he very candidly told us that the regiment meant to emigrate, as soon as it reached the town of Longuive (the last frontier town,) which they afterwards did. They had a very excellent band of music; and captain Robertson said we should have it the next evening if we pleased; certainly, was the reply. We invited all the officers in the afternoon; and I beat up for all my young female acquaintance to join the dance, and a most delightful evening we had of it; they were well pleased with their reception, and we with their company; it served for a momentary gleam of sunshine through the clouded sky that had hovered over us so long. They left us next morning; how they have been disposed of since I know not.

Soon after, one evening, I had a card party at my house, when about nine o'clock, word was brought that the king and royal family had been stopped at Varennes, in their attempt to escape from France, and that they were coming to sleep that night at Challons. The consternation is easier to be imagined than described: an elderly lady who was present, (and who had formerly belonged to the king's aunt's establishment) asked me if I had ever seen any of the royal family? I answered in the negative. "If," said she, " I should be sent for, which I think is very likely, would you come, if I send for you?" " Certainly I will," said I. The party broke up; every one's mind was harrassed, and big with conjecture as to what would be the result of that day's event.

At a few minutes before twelve o'clock, my friend, madame Bodenville, sent for me, and I got there but a very little while before the royal family arrived at the Maison-de-Lintendance, when every thing was prepared for their reception, and supper (as well as the shortness of the time, would permit.) My friend and I attended at the back of the queen's chair, with full hearts at the passing scene. The royal party consisted of the king and queen, the dauphin and madame royal, (the present duchess D'Angoulême,) and madame Elizabeth, the king's sister, (afterwards guillotined.) The king and the children ate a very good supper, but the queen and madame Elizabeth ate very little ; the tears ran down both their faces much too fast to think of eating : theirs' was food for meditation, even to madness. Oh! that I had the pen of Shakespeare to write that night's scene ; my poor pen cannot convey one thousandth part of it. The beautiful queen looked at her husband, then at her children, and then at the company that surrounded her, which was pretty much of all descriptions. Liberty had given many permission to thrust in *their faces*, who never would have *dared* to think of such a thing, had not their *king* been *assailed* by *misfortune*. She looked up to heaven, clasped her hands together, but did not speak. My tears were not to be restrained, for I really sobbed aloud, till I drew the eyes of many on me, some of them not the most benign. The queen only took a small biscuit and a glass of wine; and when things were ready, they retired to bed, I had almost said to rest. It was then near three o'clock in the morning; my friend and I retired into an adjoining room, and threw ourselves on a sofa, and talked over the great events of that night, till tired nature could hold out no longer, and we fell asleep, I may say, in spite of ourselves.

CHAPTER VI.

IN CONTINUATION.

AT eight o'clock all again was bustle and confusion; but before that time I had been home, and got a few things which the queen stood in *need of against* her rising, the family having left Paris as if to take an airing, and had very little more than what they stood upright in.

I ran no small risk in getting out and in again, for by that time the news of the king's being stopped had spread abroad; and the people from the surrounding towns and villages, were flocking in from all parts, so that by the time they had taken a little coffee, &c. for breakfast, it was time to go to chapel (the chapel was in the house); but the noise and confusion was so great, it prevented the service going on, for they were ready to tear the priest from the altar, and such was the behaviour of the mob, that the royal family were obliged to quit the chapel before the service was finished. My friend and I staid on

E

the outside, which opened on to the stair-head
at which was placed a grenadier to guard the
stair-case, (and as savage a looking fellow as I
ever saw in my life.) When the queen came out
of the chapel she had the dauphin in her arms,
the child being frightened by the noise and
tumult he had heard. The soldier made a motion
with his musquet, as if he would bayonet the
queen or the child. I lost all presence of mind,
but one, and that was to snatch the prince out of
his mother's arms, and run away with him into
the drawing-room; the queen was not angry
with me; her sorrows were too deep to be moved
by trifles; and I begged ten thousand pardons
for my impetuosity. She was standing at a small
distance from me, and she asked me what coun-
trywoman I was? I told her I had the honour
of being an Englishwoman. She immediately
came to me, and in an agony of tears, caught
hold of both my hands, saying, as well as her
sobs would let her, " Oh! madame, madame,
what would I give were I and my family in your
hospitable country; then should we be safe, and
far, far, from this turbulent people, (said she,
looking towards the street) for never, oh! never,
shall I be in safety again after this unfortunate
day." I endeavoured all I could to console her,
and bid her hope for the best, and that it would

be all well in the end ; (but it was what I did not believe myself) she shook her head mournfully, with a seeming presage of the dreadful event. The poor little dauphin kept asking her all the time why she cried so, *(pour quoi pluerez vous mama reine).** *Orders* were *given* to the *king* and *queen* to make ready to depart. I had told my husband in the morning that it was settled between my friend and me, that I should go with the royal family as far as Epérney, (the next town on the road to Paris ;) she being too infirm, and too much fatigued to go herself, and for him to get the horse and chaise ready, and I would come to him as soon as I found a proper opportunity. I just got the start of the royal family, as I had to order the preparations for the dinner; I was there long before them, as they went very slow, on account of the great number of people that surrounded them. The young men of the town took all the horses belonging to the gard de corps to the number of fifty, and some of their own, and with them formed a body guard; and it was well they did, as I am sure they would have been torn to pieces by the mob †.

---

* Why do you cry so, mamma queen?

† The people were taught to believe, that if the royal family had made their escape, that the foreign troops would.

I think I do not exaggerate when I say, I saw an hundred thousand persons, men, women, and children, armed with all sorts of instruments of destruction, and with which the royal family were threatened, hissed, and groaned at all the way. I arrived at Epérney and set the cooks to work to get them something ready as well as time would permit.

I cannot help mentioning a circumstance which took place a little before the royal family reached Eperney; as I said before, that the villages and towns, far and near, were abandoned of their inhabitants, to assemble on the great road, some out of curiosity, and some to insult the Royal Family, when there arrived in a post-chaise a gentleman and two ladies coming to the inn, at which I was standing at the window. One of the ladies was very *fair*, (and so was the queen,) and very well dressed. A countryman, with a large pitchfork in his hand, stopped the chaise, aided by more of his companions, mounted in front of it, and putting the pitchfork in (with an intent to kill the queen as he thought) fixed the fair lady by the neck, to the back of the chaise : but fortunately for her, the fork was

enter France, and burn, pillage, and destroy, would be the order of the day ; and that accounts for their very bad behaviour.

very large, so much so, as to take the neck in
between the prongs, and she received no other
injury than being half-frightened to death, and
there he held her for several minutes, till con-
vinced of his mistake by the arrival of the real
personage, for whom he *intended* that *kindness ;*
but he was prevented from doing the queen any
injury, by the guards that surrounded her.

As the queen was descending from the carriage, to set her foot in a miserable inn, one of the
many viragos, that had taken possession of the
steps and the door-way to the inn, with the most
opprobrious language, gave a snatch at the queen's
clothes, and by that means broke the string of
her pocket, which I soon repaired Little time was
given to eat the morsel prepared for them, and
the queen *(poor soul!)* through fatigue, want
of rest, and food, and still more, the great
anxiety of mind, looked half dead.

Just before leaving the inn she took a most
affectionate and sorrowful leave of me (the tears
streaming down her beautiful face, and said she
should never see me more in this world, and bid
me not forget her, and her sufferings ; but pray
for her—pray for the unfortunate Antoinette !—
Forget thee, thou poor suffering angel !—No,

never, while memory holds her place in my poor
brain ; nor shall I ever forget the twenty-four
hours I passed from the time I first saw her, till
I reached my home again.   I know not why she
noticed me so much, unless it was that she saw
I sympathised with her in her grief, and that I
was an Englishwoman.   But, to proceed, the
orders were again given for the departure of the
royal sufferers.   As the queen was getting into
the carriage, she looked around, and saw the
woman who had insulted her, and she gave her
a Louis-d'or, saying, at the same time, " Take
that, woman; it is to buy thy children bread
with ; it is a pity *they* should suffer for the *bad
conduct of their mother."* The woman held
down her head abashed, and in a moment was
lost among the crowd.   The cavalcade moved on,
and I saw the queen no more.

The young men who had formed the guard,
did not intend, when they set out, going further
than Epérney : but when they saw the gross and
cruel treatment that the royal family had met
with, and were likely to meet with on the road,
they formed the resolution of not quitting their
majesties, till they arrived in Paris, nor did they.

Since my return to England, I have had the honour of being in the presence of the Duchess D'Angoulême, and alone with her in her bed-chamber; but my feelings would not let me re-mind her of that eventful day, lest I should open afresh those wounds, but ill-closed, and revive again her grief for her murdered parents.

I found myself greatly fatigued, and should have been glad to have stopped that night at Epérney, but courier succeeded courier, with intelligence that the Austrian troops, with the marshal Duke de Broglio at their head, had entered the town of Chàllons, with fire and sword destroying all before them, which alarmed us very much, as all the little property we had in France, such as clothes, &c. &c. was at their mercy. We talked the matter over, and though we were afraid that the road would not be very safe after such a day, yet, we thought it would be better to know the worst, than stay fretting there all night.

The distance we had to go was twenty-one miles, and it was near nine o'clock when we set off. As we went along, we had strong reason to suspect that our horse had been cheated of his corn, and we were obliged to stop to give him a feed, by the time we had gone six miles. At the house where we stopped, we unfortunately met with about twenty return carts, that had brought the people that day from the surrounding villages. The drivers of these carts were half drunk with wine, and half mad with politics; and just in right trim for any mischief that might present. We did not much like their looks; as they were going our road, we had rather not have travelled with them.

The landlord informed us they would turn off the road at about six miles distant; they set out, and we stopped till near midnight, when we thought, of course, we should not see them again; but we overtook them; they were noisy and insolent; that we took no notice of. (It is one of the finest roads in all France, all gravel and very wide; there was plenty of room for us to pass on either side of them.) As they chose to keep exactly the middle, and we had passed them all, to about four or five, when one of the drivers took it in his head that we should not pass. I was driving, as my husband could not very well see at night. He flogged his great cart horses, (there were three to each cart) and they set off at a gallop, and were as mad as their masters. There was no time for reflection: I whipped my horse, which was a very spirited one, and away he went. At the same time, I was obliged to whip *their horses* over the head to keep them *off from us ;* and I can safely say, that there were moments when I did not know on which side we should upset. I gained ground on them, amidst the vilest oaths and execrations they could think of, and pelting us behind with the gravel that lay by the road side ; but that we did not care for, as there was a hood to the chaise ; but it shewed their malignity. And I have no doubt, that if any one among them had proposed to have murdered us that night, that the others would have consented. And thus we made a running fight of it for about three miles. We got home safe, between two and three in the morning, and found neither fire, or soldiers, (nor had there been any) or any one inclined to be more mischievous than our own people, who were by *that time* pretty well *tired* of that day's exploits.

I cannot conclude this chapter without making a reflection on the mutability of all human grandeur. The first time the unfortunate queen of France passed through Chlàlons was on her marriage with the dauphin of France, on her way to Paris to meet her husband and future king ; * the *last* time was on the day the Royal

---

* On her marriage with the dauphin, the town of Chàllons raised a triumphal arch at one of the entrances into the town, in honour of her, and called it the Port Dauphine.

Family had been stopped at Varennes; and 'she passed *again* under the triumphal arch on her way to Paris, and a little while afterwards, to a tribunal, and from thence to the guillotine.— *Oh, tempora! oh, mores!*

CHAPTER VII.

PRINCE PAUL D'ESTERHAZY'S REGIMENT OF HORSE
LAPIDATED THROUGH THE TOWN OF CHALLONS
SUR MARNE.

VERY soon after the return of the royal family to
Paris, all foreign regiments in the pay of France,
gave great offence to the great nation, as it was
then called; and in particular that fine regiment
Prince D'Esterhazy's (he was first cousin to the
queen of France.) They were ordered to leave
Paris immediately, and France as soon as possible, to which the prince had no objection, only
that he knew he was leaving his cousin in the
hands of her mortal enemies; but he was obliged
to submit, having no power to resist.

They made forced marches: how far they had
come the day they reached Chàllons, I know
not; but they had been travelling from four
o'clock in the morning. While on their march,
there was a courier sent before them, offering a
thousand Louis d'ors for securing the person of
prince D'Esterhazy, dead or alive. The prince
in all probability was apprised, that such a thing

was likely to take place, and it was supposed, afterwards, that he had disguised himself as one of the private troopers. Be that as it may, it might be so, and it may have been known to the whole regiment, but not a man among them (to their honour be it spoken) but would have defended his prince and commander to the last of his existence.

The moment it was known in Chàllons that the regiment was expected, the people assembled in a most riotous manner, declaring, that they should not enter the town; for which purpose they took possession of the only gate by which they could enter, the *Port-de-Marne*. The troops could not ford the river, and they had no other road to gain the frontier than through the town of Chàllons; therefore, all they could do was to wait patiently till something was done to let them in. They several times attempted to parley with those in possession of the gate; but the only answer they received was a volley of stones and rubbish. They had been more than two hours exposed to a scorching sun, in the dog days, and it was then near four o'clock in the afternoon. At length all the respectable inhabitants seeing no end to the insults offered to this unfortunate regiment, cried shame on the

supineness of the mayor and magistrates, who
could thus suffer the rabble-rout to do just as
they pleased. At last, after a good deal of alter-
cation, the mayor, *well accompanied*, sallied
forth, and insisted upon the gates being opened;
if not, for the soldiers to remain in the town that
night, at least, to let them pass through it; they
agreed, on condition of their not stopping, and
they were suffered to come in accordingly; but
it was under a heavy shower of stones and dirt,
and the regiment passed through the town at full
charge, (or as the French call it, *venter-a-terre.)*
The people shouted and pelted them from the
houses, and the house-tops, as they passed along.
The ground trembled under the horses' feet; the
fire flew from their shoes; the noise of the people
—the gallopping of the horses—and all together,
for the time it lasted, was one of the most terrific
scenes I ever saw. Having gained the outside of
the town, they drew up, when most of the inhabitants sent them provisions both for man and
horse, (and not before they wanted it, poor
creatures) as we found that they had both of them
been without any food for near fourteen hours.
Many of the men were so angry and enraged
that they refused every thing for themselves, but
took for their poor horses, whose bowels roared
from wind and emptiness, most tremendously.

We had followed our servant, whom we had sent with a hamper of provisions, and just as we came up to him, we found him offering one of the men to eat, which he most disdainfully refused. I took a loaf of bread and a bottle of wine, and asked the trooper, in English, if he would not take it from an Englishwoman?—(He was a fine man; but from his angry countenance and his large black whiskers, he looked most ferocious.) He looked at me with marked surprise; and repeated " English, English!" " Yes," said I; when he instantly seized it (and I may say devoured it.) Some others of his companions joined with him, and they soon emptied the hamper, when one of them with a smile on his face, and in the French language, thanked me.

. They slept that night as well as they could, in a long straggling village near the town. To the best of my recollection, there might be about four hundred men, enough to have set fire to our town, if it had pleased them so to do; but that would have been bad policy, as they had many larger towns to go through than ours; and they, in that case, would never have got out of the country alive; as it was, I believe, they lost some men, at least it was so reported. And thus ended that day, fortunately without bloodshed, if I except one of the poor fellows who had his cheek laid open with part of a glass bottle that had been thrown at him, as he galloped through the street. I think in my life, I never saw so fine a body of men, taking them all together: the officers were uncommon handsome men—most of them fair.

CHAPTER VIII.

SAVING THE LIFE OF A YOUNG IRISHMAN.

THE troops were again concentrating themselves in our town, in order to prevent the duke of Brunswick, at the head of fifty thousand men, from marching to Paris (why they did not *Dumourrier* must know best.) We had made preparations to receive the duke in our house, (which was a very handsome one) and being the only English family in the place, we flattered ourselves we should have had the honour of receiving him; we had also made up our minds to leave France, had the allies advanced, as the rear of the army would have opened the way for us to get out; but our hopes were kept alive for ten days, without effect, when one day we had an alert in earnest. *Dumourrier,* who commanded the French army, fell back upon our town, and retired behind the Márne, (that is to say, crossed the river) and took a position on a height called St. Michael's, which commanded the town and the whole of the adjacent country; here he

planted a battery of an hundred pieces of cannon, with furnaces for making the balls red hot,
to fire on the town, had the Prussians advanced.
The bridge over the Márne, (a very fine one,
and had not been built many years) was ordered
to be cut down if the enemy came on. All the
corn was to be thrown into the river, and all
the men capable of bearing arms were ordered
to join the camp St. Michael. Fortunately for
us, the Prussians did not make their appearance,
if they had, our ramparts would not have kept
them out, for they might have been (comparatively speaking) knocked down with roasted
apples, and the town burnt by the French army,
from the heights. Thus stationed between two
fires we should have been in a hopeful plight.

Just in the midst of all the confusion of
evacuating the town, a young man was brought
in by the country people, who found him wan-
dering about the fields, with the uniform of De
Walshe's regiment. He had a musket slung
across his shoulders, which the people took from
him, and were going to kill him with the butt-end
of it, when all the French he could muster was,
" Deserté, deserté ;" upon which they desisted,
and brought him to the Town Hall. A general
officer was there (who had served with La

G

Fayette in America) who spoke a little English, he asked the young man some questions, and found he was a volunteer, just arrived in France, going to join the regiment of De Walshe, to which he was attached, but having lost his way, and not speaking the French language, was picked up by the country people, as before described. There was no time for ceremony; the general thought the best thing he could do was to send the young man to our house; he did so, but it was near costing us our lives. As soon as the town was evacuated, the people, consisting of old men, women, and mischievous boys, began to assemble on the market place, and talk of the *spy*, as they called him; and what made it worse both for him and for us, was that they knew by his uniform he belonged to De Walshe's regiment, which regiment they also knew had emigrated, and had joined the army De Condé, therefore nothing would satisfy their vengeance, but they must have his life! They came in a body of at least two hundred (there was not a magistrate left in the town, and all law and authority was at an end) to demand him, saying, that if we refused him, they would pull down the house, or set fire to it, and that they should consider us no better than the spy, whom we protected. What was to be done

in this dilemma? We could not think of resign-
ing him into the hands of the mob; that would
be giving him up to certain death. My husband
proposed to go and speak to them; but he speaking the French language badly, that would not
do. While we were thus debating, the poor
young man was in agony, begging that we would
not run the risk of our lives, to save his, but let
him go to them. That, all the laws of honour
and humanity forbade. We were so long in
coming to a decision of what was best to be done,
that we expected every moment they would break
the gates down and come to us. At last it was
decided, that if I went to them, they might be
less inclined to insult a woman than a man, so I
took courage (which, thank God, never deserted
me at my need) and went to them. I had the
small gate opened, and I held up my hand, and
begged their attention. (I know not whether it
was the idea of endeavouring to save the life of a
fellow-creature and countryman, or that some
benign power assisted me; but certain it is, that
I was eloquent in his defence.) I told them,
among other things, that so far was *he* from being
their enemy, that he was their *friend*. (One and
all, how was that?) I will tell you, if you will
listen to me: "When he left his native country
it was to join De Walshe's regiment, he being a

Catholic, (I took great care to lay a stress on the word *Catholic*) then in the service of France; but when he had gained the frontier, on finding that the regiment had deserted, he was so *indignant* and so *shocked* at the *treacherous* conduct of the regiment, that he immediately turned towards France, with a determination to serve the *patrie*—her and her only."—" Bravo! bravo!" They did not know that he was so fine a fellow, or that I was so good a woman : although ten minutes before that, they would have thought no more of making a *good woman* of me, (in the vulgar acceptation of the word) than they would of cutting off the head of a chicken. I retired, amidst loud huzzas, well pleased at having got so well rid of my troublesome visitors. Not that we were too much at our ease; the times were too liable to change; what was patriotism one day, was high treason the next.

At this time we were eight days without bread in the town. Potatoes was a vegetable very little known, and less used by the French; but we were in the habit of eating them, whenever we could get any, and I had laid in a few for fear of accidents, but my *servants* would not *eat them,* and asked me if I took them for *pigs !* but *pigs,* or not *pigs,* they were obliged to eat them, at that time, or go without any thing in the shape of bread. Our young protigee found no difficulty in *eating them*; and I saw him smile, more than once, when he saw the potatoes brought to table in the *true Irish* way, with their *jackets on*.

CHAPTER IX.

IN CONTINUATION.

As the enemy did not advance, which they were not much in a condition to do ; as the French, prior to their leaving that side of the country, had cut off all the springs of water that served the Prussian camp; so that man and horse died for want of it ; and to add to the misfortune, the men gathered and eat the unripe grapes, which killed many thousands of them.   It was reported that the Prussians lost thirty-thousand men on the plains of Champaign, without firing a shot. I know for a certainty, that long after both camps were broken up, and that so late in the year as the end of October, we made a party to go and see the Prussian encampment, near the town of Montolone, called the *Camp-de-la-Lune;*

but when we were at the distance of two leagues from it, the smell was so offensive, from the many bodies that the earth barely covered, and the great number of horses yet undevoured on the plain, that we could not proceed any further.— Our townspeople came back from the camp St. Michael, and the intercourse between the town and the country was again restored.

The general officer, who sent the young man to us, called to consult what was best to be done for our young friend. He well knew how he was situated, and felt for him. The general seemed to be a most amiable man ; but like many others, obliged, in order to save his family and his property, to join with the strongest side. He said that the Irish college still existed in Paris, and he would write to them. He did so, and in about a fortnight the young man left us ; we had furnished him with every thing he had wanted during the time he staid with us. He said he had only thanks to give us for our support and protection, in a moment so pregnant with danger ; and with tears of gratitude running down his face, he bade us adieu ! hoping God would reward us for our kindness to him.

We afterwards heard that he had arrived safe

at the college, and that they had found means to get him out of the country, and we never heard more of him. His name, to the best of my recollection, was Roberts, or a name very like it. He belonged to a very respectable Catholic family in Cork.

CHAPTER X.

DEATH OF THE KING OF FRANCE.

AFTER that melancholy affair of the tenth of August, the king and royal family were shut up in the Temple, the Republic was proclaimed, the royal authority put down in every thing, even to the fleur-de-lis struck off from the gates and walls; and every thing wearing the most serious and alarming aspect. And though I had been accustomed to many alarms, yet my mind seemed harassed and worn out. To look back was horror; to look forward, all was dark and uncertain. I saw no end to our continual fears and changes. Every day the state of the country was getting worse and worse, and the specimen they had already given us of Republican principles, was not at all to our liking, and we thought if there was any possibility of getting out of the country, that the sooner we did it the better; but we were informed that no permission to leave

H

the country could be obtained but by personal
application in Paris.

Under this idea we arranged all our affairs,
and set off for Paris in the month of January,
1793, and arrived on the 17th, the very day on
which the Assemble National had voted the
death of *Louis Seize*—(here was a new scene
for us, who were endeavouring to fly from it.)
All Paris was astonished and confounded (but she
had not then risen to that pre-eminence in crime
she afterwards attained.)   On the night before
the death of the king, my husband was stopped,
at ten o'clock, by six men, demanding of him
to what party he belonged? " Gentlemen," said
he, " I am of no party—I am an Englishman."
" Oh! pass, Monsieur."   (What a dreadful
question, when put to a Frenchman at such a
moment.)   We had taken lodgings in the Rue
St. Honoré, not far from the Palais Royal.   The
dreadful morn arrived of the 21st of January—
the drums beat to arms—the cannons rolled along
the streets—a dead silence was observed by every
one that passed. 1 had wrapped myself up
warm, and was seated outside of the window on
the balcony, to observe and contemplate the
passing scene. The consternation of the people
exceeded all description ; the shops were not

permitted to be shut; no one was suffered to leave his work; every thing was to go on as if nothing was amiss. Even the very theatres were not suffered to be closed, but they were very thinly attended. The people went into the shops, and from what I could see from my post, came out again without making a purchase. In short, the whole of the scene before me, brought forcibly to my mind the description given by Hubert to king John, of the death of Prince Arthur, and to that I must refer my readers; but I saw realised, that which Shakespeare saw in his mind's eye only. There were about forty thousand men in Paris that day, who carried arms in favour of the king. Had he been permitted to speak to his subjects, surely there could not be a man amongst them who could have withstood his king on a scaffold, pleading to them for *protection* and *mercy*. The moment he was about to address them, that *wretch* SANTARE— that *brewer* of small *beer* and *mischief*, ordered the drums to beat, and the executioner to do his duty—in an instant the *deed* was *done* passed *all human recall*. The night before the death of the king one of the deputies of the Convention was assassinated, Lepeltier St. Fargaux (and I believe in my conscience one of the best amongst them.) The day after the death of the king, by way of taking off the attention of the Parisians, for fear they should think too much of their murdered sovereign. Lepeltier was carried openly along the streets on a bed of repose, with a garland of laurel round his head, the sheet turned down below the stomach, exhibiting a sabre wound under the left breast, of the length of my middle finger. The scheme succeeded to their wish, and the thoughts of the *thoughtless multitudes* were turned from one object to another. The people had been told, that it was the king's party that had put that good man to death, which made them cry " Shame! shame! on the perpetrators of so foul a deed!" " So I say, it was a foul deed, but no one shall ever make me believe that it was not done by those most in power ; the police of Paris is too good for such a thing to escape its vigilance, and the man or men were never found out who did it.

You will say we had not much mended our quarters ; that is true, but we lived in hopes of getting our passport ; but time passed away, and we were no better off. Various changes and revolutions took place ; and we were often called up in the middle of the night to shew our papers ; and to see if the account which we gave of ourselves at different places, agreed one with another. Indeed, no one could live in Paris, or any part of the kingdom, without a sort of personal protection, which you were obliged to carry about with you, describing your height, your age, the colour of your hair and eyes, and so exact, that no one could mistake one person for another.

About this time we went one evening to the play at Lapetit Montensieur, (a small play-house in the Palais Royal) when we were much surprised on coming out to find that we were prisoners. The gates of the Palais Royal were all shut, and we were obliged to remain there till our papers were examined by the proper authorities. We did not give them much trouble; they set their marks upon them, and we were told to pass on, and though we lodged not two hundred yards from the place, we did not get home till past two in the morning (*Vive la Liberte!*) But we left numbers behind us, who were not so fortunate as ourselves; and, indeed, I am much afraid many who never saw their homes again, as there were more than eight hundred persons taken up that night, and sent to the different prisons, who were no doubt of the number of those unfortunate victims, who suffered on the first and second of September following. In the course of those two days upwards of four thousand persons suffered on the scaffold, known by the name of the "Septembresuers," or *emptying the prisons*, as it was called.

We still remained in Paris making daily applications for our passports, but to no pupose; they still kept guillotining the people in all directions! I remember going out one morning in particular, when having occasion to cross the Place de Carousal. I went on, not knowing there had been an execution that day, though there was only a small street between us (but such was the frequency of those things, that we knew nothing about it till it was all over) and they were *sweeping* and *strewing* the ground with *saw-dust* to *hide appearances*. They were grown so expert at it, that the day I am speaking of, they had guillotined *sixteen* people in *fourteen* minutes!

Then came the famous 31st of May (when the Jacobins got the better of the Rowlandins, and the Bresotonians, and when the decree was carried by a great majority against the thirty-one Deputies who would not sign the death of the king: they were to be sent into exile to an island in the South Seas.) I never went to bed that night; I passed the whole of it on the balcony. I was afraid to go to bed, as no one knew how it might end.

The whole of the Guard National were under arms, parading up and down the street, two and two on both sides, the cannon rolling in the middle with lighted match, ready for action, till the signal was given about six o'clock in the morning that they were no longer necessary: for by this time the Assemblée National (soon afterwards denominated the Convention) had carried their votes against the Deputies, and had secured their persons. I also saw go by to suffer, the famous Charlotte Cordy. * She showed a courage that would have done honour to the most valiant hero of antiquity.

We went so constantly for our passports, that at length we tired them out, and they told us they would give us one for any part of France, but not to leave the country. In consequence finding we could not get away, we fixed upon Amiens, and we left Paris on the 24th of June, 1793, consoling ourselves with having got somewhat nearer to England, but for the power of reaching it, we might as well have been at the North Pole.

---

* Who assassinated Marat.

CHAPTER XI.

THE ARREST OF THE ENGLISH AFTER THE AFFAIR OF QUIBERON.

WE arrived at Amiens, and having settled ourselves tolerably comfortable, we enjoyed a tem-
porary calm from all the noise and confusion of
Paris ; but, alas! the calm was of short dura-
tion, and served to make us feel the storm the
more severely. The expedition to Quiberon,
and failure, brought down that terrible decree
against all the English residing in France. All
those that lived at Lisle, Calais, Arras, &c. &c.
were brought to be shut up in Amiens, in different
old convents, allotted for that purpose as prisons.
Whole respectable families, fathers, mothers,
and children, with only a matrass or two and a
blanket, with not more than a change of clothes,
and some of them not that, brought away from
their residences in the middle of the night, hur-
ried away in carts with a bundle or two of straw
to sit on; in fact, not much unlike what we see

now and then in England, when removing pau-
pers from one parish to another. We that were
in the town fared somewhat better, as we had a
little more time given us for preparation. We
took but few things with us, not supposing but
what we should soon be out again, having committed no crime—but the honour of being born
in England was crime enough in their eyes. The
seals were put on those things left in our houses
and lodgings, which we had to pay the rent for,
just the same as if we lived in them. *(Vive la
Justice!)* But in the confusion of the moment,
I hardly know what I took, or what I left, and
that will easily be believed, when I say, that in
going to prison, the husbands and wives were
separated, in the most unfeeling manner; to
have suffered us to be confined in the same
prison, would have been thought too great a
luxury by those refiners in villainy!

In the first prison I was in (I was in four different ones, and returned to one of them again)
I was put in a room in which were seven women;
the room might be about sixteen by fourteen
feet. We all had a camp bedstead, mattrass, and
bedding each, but for chairs or table, that was
quite out of the question. Our dinner, if we
had the means of paying for it, (for it was literally

point *d'argent point Swiss)* was brought to us ready cooked. Some of the ladies put the dinner on the beds and knelt down while eating it ; but as I was not a *Catholic,* my knees did not like the position ; so I sat on the bed-side, and put the plate on my knees, and in this way we managed, as well as we could, for four or five days, before we got either chair or table, which we obtained at last by hiring them ; but what was a great trouble to us, was, that the dirty fellows that were placed at the gate of the house as guards, used to put their nasty fingers into our plate of victuals. If they thought it was possible to convey a letter in it, or under what the dish contained (which by the ,bye, was sometimes the case, as under an omelette, for example.)

The vexations which we were continually exposed to, are not to be described. I am sure if I was to enumerate half of them, my readers might think I was exaggerating : but I must not forget to observe, that when the Republic was beaten, we were sure to feel the effects of it, by the more than usual severity of the guards at the gates ; and as we could not learn what was passing outside the walls of our *mansion,* we at last got so accustomed to their manœuvres, that we could give a pretty good guess when the French had the worst of it, and when on the contrary. We never could pass a letter without its being opened, or pretending to examine it; and I have very often seen a letter upside down in the guard's hand. In consequence of that, when writing to my husband, I used to write with very wide lines in French, and interline it with English, and it passed; for they could read *one* just as *well* as the other, unless one of their principal officers was in the way, and they took care not to trouble themselves more than they could help it. I was cautious; I did not write any thing that could get us into trouble, if they found us out.

CHAPTER XIII.

CUTTING DOWN THE TREE OF LIBERTY.

LE BONE, the deputy of Arras, was trying all he
could to get the command of Amiens, to obtain
which, it was necessary to vilify our deputy,
André Dumont, by saying that he was as great
an Aristocrat as those under his care ; and the
reason why he said so was, because the guillotine was not on *permanent* duty in our *town*, as
it was in his *(Arras)*, and that the prisoners
were as well satisfied as it was possible to be,
under all the circumstances, (we knew we could
be worse off) but at that time it was necessary
for a man to be cried out against, and noted for
his villainy and shedding of blood, to be thought
a good patriot.

We were much alarmed early one morning by
a sudden influx of about two hundred fresh prisoners, brought into our house, though by far
too full already. The poor people thus brought

in were of the very lowest class, chiefly composed of old women and others who sold fruit and vegetables in the market-place, and who in a *few days* added very much to *our misery* by the *addition* of the *company* they *brought* with *them.* If feeling for the misfortunes of others is any alleviation of one's own, certainly we felt for those poor people, as many of them had husbands, wives, and children, from whom they had been torn, waiting and crying in vain for the daily sustenance procured by the labour of those so cruelly kept from them; but they were the *Mobility,* and not the *Nobility ;* and they were let out again in the course of a week.

The Tree of Liberty had been planted with very great ceremony in the middle of the market-place, and to cut it down was the highest crime that could be committed, and could not have been done by any one, but some enemy to the *Patrie.* We (the prisoners) never had but one opinion on that subject, and that was, that André Dumont had cut it down himself, on purpose to give him an opportunity of making a great noise, and great cry out against him, for confining so many people, all of which had the desired effect; and André Dumont had well *merited* of the *Patrie* mention *honorable* and *insertion en bulletin.* Le Bone had been doing every thing in his power to supersede André Dumont, and get possession of our town, which, if he had, he would have treated us worse than the inhabitants of Arras; that is to say, he would have put twice as many to death in Amiens as he had done in Arras, such was his enmity towards our town.

After having passed the winter in this miserable abode, (for such it really was) we were ordered to prepare, one day, to take up a new abode the next. The parting from our friends in adversity, whom tyranny had promiscuously thrown together, and misfortune had endeared to each other, was truly painful, and not to be done without shedding tears. Some of us had the pleasure of meeting again, and some not.

My new lodgings were a little more roomy, and, being near the ramparts, more airy. Here I had the pleasure of meeting with my husband; he too had changed his abode; but happiness is not the lot of mortals! Here again I had a new misfortune to contend with. The sun's genial influence was just beginning to be felt, and all nature was vivified by his rays, when it pleased him to move (I may say) millions of bugs, which were clustered in the four corners of a white-

washed room, of which I was mistress, and they
visited us at night with most devouring energy!
á-la-François, sans ceremonie, *i. e.* they were
intolerable. After a great deal of labour in
cleansing the room, and incessant perseverance,
we got the better of our depredating adversaries.
At the end of two months, being as comfortable
as our local situation would admit of, we received
a fresh *rout,* and we were marched off to the
convent *De la Providence,* in which were no less
than nine hundred persons; but in that too, as
in every thing, they shewed their ingenuity in
tormenting those whom they had in their power,
by putting so many together in one building.
The men slept in large rooms—some thirty,
some forty, some more, some less, according as
they could stow them. The women and children
were too happy not to have more than six or seven
in a room. I had the supreme happiness of being
in a good sized room with some ladies of the first
distinction in France, and we, the favoured few,
were only five in a room.

CHAPTER XIV.

A SUDDEN SURPRISE.

THE ladies who lived in the same room with me, were Madame la Countess de Choisuel Goufier, and her two beautiful daughters; and a Madame de Montolon. (Why I am particular in mentioning these personages will be seen hereafter.) It would have been contrary to orders for any of the prisoners to have dared to fasten their room door either by night or by day, for if any of our *masters* had come, and found it fast, they would have immediately concluded that we had been plotting treason against the Republic, and for which reason they never let us know when they were coming. The mayor and a party of the district had paid us a visit but the day before the circumstance took place, which I am going to relate. The Countess de Choisuel had been given to understand by a friend, that if she could get a letter written (and get it out of that house that they would get it conveyed to her husband.) The Count, with two of his sons, were at that time serving in the Army de Condé.) Some days had passed since she had received that intimation, and she was anxious to take the first opportunity that offered, and she thought this a good one, as the inspectors of the prisons had been so lately (only the day before.) In consequence she sat down to write. The young ladies, with Madame de Montolon, went to walk, and as I had a piece of work in hand, which I was anxious to finish, I sat down also Madame might have written about one side of a sheet of paper, when in an instant away flew the door wide open and, to our astonished view, there stood before us André Dumont, the mayor, and the whole of the district. We never stirred from our seats, (which is contrary to the custom, of the country, and all good breeding.) Dumont quick as lightning, perceived there was something wrong. He advanced to the table, saying, with a tone of authority, " Let me see, Citizen, to whom you are writing," at the same time laying hold of the paper—(fortunately Madame had not power to attempt to hide it)—and read aloud, " My dear Madame, (a name he invented) if you have any thing very new, and very pretty in Paris in the cap way, do, pray send me one."

K

" *Nonsense,*" *replied he,* " what can a woman want with new-fashioned caps while shut up in a prison !" and while he was speaking he tore the letter to atoms, and threw it in the fire-place, turned on his heel and left us, to our unspeakable relief. Madame instantly burst into tears, fell on her knees, made the sign of the cross, and thanked God for her deliverance. I was almost as much frightened as she was; but it was on her account, as it rested entirely with the deputy. Her life was in his hands, and he could have ordered her to be guillotined that instant in Amiens, or send her to Paris, which he pleased, as she was detected in holding a correspondence with the enemies of the Republic, which was death by the law. It is quite certain that nothing but the humanity of the man, and his great presence of mind, could have saved her. I left the room telling her I would send her daughters to her, which I did. I then went in search of my husband, to relate to him what a fright we had been in ; but that was nothing compared to what followed a very little time after.

We were dreadfully alarmed in the middle of the night by our prison being filled with soldiers, some bearing arms, some torches, the light of which striking upon the bayonets, the whole

place seemed (amid the smoke) to be on fire!—
All must get up instantly—the nobles were to be
separated from the non-nobles, and the men from
the women: Here my pen faulters in attempting
to give any thing like a description—I must leave
it to the imagination of my readers to do justice
to the scene that followed, when I have informed
them, that nothing was to be heard but screams,
groans, and sobs, for they thought that they were
all to be sent to Paris, and that the same dreadful
scenes were to be acted over again that had taken
place the September before. Husbands and
wives, fathers, mothers, and children, hanging
on the necks of each other, thinking the last
moment of their lives was come, and that they
should never see one another more. None but
the hearts of Republicans could see such a sight
unmoved, which they did, though I allow they
were obliged to do their duty; yet, they might
have done it with less brutality, at least we
thought so at the time.

By the same rule, I again was separated from
my husband; he was marched off to another
prison, and I was left in that.

The convent *De la Providence* was a very
large building, and our ranks had been so woefully

K 2

thinned in the last *skirmish* we had had with the *enemy*, that what with losing my husband and most of my acquaintance, with whom I used to associate, the deserted and melancholy walls made the horrors of a prison doubly felt'; so much so, that I fell ill, and was apprehensive of a violent fever, but it turned out only what the French call a *fievre-d'ennui.* The secretary belonging to the district was a very good young man, and was very attentive to the prisoners, and was the means very often, of obtaining comforts for them which no other person had in their power to do so well ; and he was particularly attentive to the English ; so I thought I could not do better than state my case to him, and begged of him to get me removed to the *Hotel Dieu,* * that I thought I should be much better there than where I was ; he busied himself for me, and in the course of two or three days after I had first spoken to him, he succeeded.

---

* The common sick hospital of the town before the Revolution.

CHAPTER XIV.

ON EQUALITY.

THE first three nights after I went to my new habitation, I was under the necessity of sleeping in the Female Dormitory, in which were twenty women. That was any thing but pleasant, and little conducive to health. I found that the mayor was charged with the management of that house and its inmates ; so I stood watch for his coming, which he did every morning. I represented to him the very bad state of my health, and begged if he could let me have some place less objectionable, that I should be very much obliged to him, &c. I pleaded very hard, and at last he said he would see what he could do for me, and the next morning he was as good as his word, and I had the *supreme happiness* of being mistress of a room all to myself. It is true, it was not very large ; it was about fourteen feet long, by six wide ; the window commanded a very fine view over the gardens ; the air and

light was good; and although my husband was
not at that house, yet the society of my old
friends and acquaintances soon had the desired
effect, and I got quite well.

It may not be amiss in this place to make an
observation, that although our Representative
(member of the Convention) took a most *ex-
traordinary* way of *proceeding*, that of ter-
rifying us so in the middle of the night; yet,
he succeeded in making a *selection* of the prisoners, which he could not have made in any
other way with *safety* to *himself*, for certainly
the *Hotel Dieu* was the prison by pre-eminence,
and happy he or they that could obtain it (as a
prison) for by this time the *Law Agréger* (every
thing in common) was put in force, and the
Great Nation took possession of the property of
those that were emigrated, and also of those that
were in prison; but then the nation *fed those
that were in prison* at *their expense* (the nation's,
as it was called) and those that had not any means
of living, lived at the expense of those that had.
(So much for the Law Agréger.)

There was in that house a very large room,
known in all convents by the name of the Re-
fectory, or General Eating Room, in which were

placed four or five large tables, big enough to dine thirty or forty people at each : at the head of each table was placed one of the greatest personages in the prison; and we all sat down to dinner like so many children at school; and as we were placed the first day, by the mayor, so we ever after took our seats.

I had the honour of being at the first table, at the head of which was Monseigneur le Duc, and Madame la Duchesse de Beuveron, and Madame de Boisgelain, their daughter, and Mademoiselle de Boisgelain, and two Englishmen, (the two Mr. Dawsons of Manchester) and several other persons I do not remember. But I must not forget, that the valet-de-chambre de Monseigneur le Due, and *la femme de chambre de Madame la Duchesse,* had the honour of dining at the same table with their *Lord* and *Lady, equality* being the *order* of the *day.* The *Duc de Beuveron* was supposed to be one of the proudest men in all France, and could *ill brook* such treatment at *his table,* and yet he was to consider it as an *indulgence* granted to him, in having those at *his* table, whose sentiments were well known ; and as to his servants being placed at the same table with him, that was merely to keep up the *farce* of *equality ;* but the

Duke for all that, was determined to keep up *his dignity,* for he very seldom opened his lips.

At the next table was placed Madame la Countess de Choiseul, and her two charming daughters ; who there were else I know not, if I except a man who, I am ashamed to say, was an Englishman, but whose name I do not remember bu t a greater demagogue never crossed the Channel. At the next table below him sat his counter-part, a Colonel Keating—of him I shall have occasion to speak hereafter ; and I shall only add, that the English who gave in to the Revolution, who stiled themselves *French Patriots,* were most cordially detested by the French Revolutionists themselves ; as they could not allow of a man's *sincerity* in *their cause,* when he abandoned and *reviled his own* country.

CHAPTER XV.

A SHORT CHAPTER ON FEMALE CURIOSITY.

ONE day after dinner (the weather being extremely hot) I was walking about the house in a loitering mood, when I saw a door open, which led out of the house, that I had never seen before, (no doubt left open by mistake); when a little *female curiosity* induced me to see where it led to. Not under any idea of getting away, that would have been madness ; besides, there was a point of *honour* among the *prisoners*, that not *one* of them should attempt to get away, as that would have subjected the *rest* to very great severities. When I saw a long narrow court with folding gates at the bottom, and in the court were laying

L

ten or a dozen casks of wine, which had apparently come in that day. Directly opposite to where I stood, I saw another door, into which I looked and saw it was a sort of kitchen garden, and no doubt belonging to that house, but then it had a very fine gravel walk, and what had that to do in a kitchen garden. While I was making these observations and reflections to myself, I was looking about, and I neither saw or heard any one; so on I went, determined to see where this fine gravel walk led to. I had got about half way down, when I thought I heard voices. I stopped—all again was quiet—I saw something like a summer-house to the left of me—but I still kept going on, till I came right in front of it, when, to my great astonishment, I saw a large table set out with all sorts of good things, such as cold chickens, ham, salad, tarts, creams, fruits, &c. &c. and wine in abundance, with about a dozen men sitting at it. I was struck motionless—so were they—I made an attempt to retreat; but one of them put up his hand for me to stop. A little recovered from our mutual surprise, I begged their pardon for the intrusion, and assured them that I did not know that any one was in the garden when I entered it. My little old friend the mayor (for it was no less than the whole of the district, with the mayor at the head of them, regaling themselves in the afternoon, at the expense of the Great Nation) got up and laid hold of my hand, " What !" said he, " has brought my little Englishwoman here !" at the same time drawing me towards the table, but I would not sit down—I told him with a great deal of naiveté, that I had found the door open, and that curiosity had led me there. I again attempted to withdraw. " No ! no !" said he, (still keeping hold of my hand) " you shall not get off so, neither ; I will not let you go, but on two conditions only." " What be they," said I, " First, that you will drink a glass of wine with us, (and he filled one out, which I drank to all their healths) and now, said he, the next is, that you will promise me, and all of us present, on the word and honour of an Englishwoman, that you never mention in *this house* what you have seen here this day." I gave him my word of honour that I never would, nor I never did, and away I ran, vowing at the same time, that curiosity should never lead me into such a scrape again ; but I could not help making the remark while drinking the wine, that they did not drink the worst wine that was brought to the house ; they would have been fools if they had ; it was all the same in the end—the Great Nation paid for all.

I should not have troubled my readers with this, to them uninteresting adventure, had it not been for what took place a little time after, and which circumstance I have no doubt was ultimately the means of saving my life, as will be seen in the next chapter.

CHAPTER XVI.

IN DANGER OF BEING GUILLOTINED FOR SINGING "GOD
SAVE THE KING" WHILE IN PRISON.

ONE day after dinner (we dined at two o'clock)
the weather being so intensely hot, we could not
walk out. The long passages belonging to the
house, were by far the coolest places we could
find. The Ladies de Choisuel, and another
French Lady, the two Mr. Dawsons and myself,
were all going up stairs at the same time; my
room being near the stair-head, I opened the
door, and asked the Ladies if they would walk in
and rest themselves; (and of course I included the
whole of the company.) The Ladies laughed at
the idea of six people sitting down in so small a
room with only *one chair* in it, but I told them
that the side and foot of my bedstead must supply the rest; so down we sat. The window and

door were left open, and by that means we got an agreeable breath of air.

The spirits of a Frenchwoman are always buoyant, and some of the Ladies began singing (like so many birds in a cage) and then another, and so on. When one of them turned to me and said, " I have often heard talk of your national air, but I never heard it; I should like very much to hear it." I replied I would do my best towards it with a great deal of pleasure, and turning to the two Mr. Dawsons, asked them if they would not make a trio of it; they said they would try, and we did so, and we sang " God save the King," probably with more glee than we might have done had we been in England. Busy fancy had wafted us to our native shore, and we forgot, for a few minutes, that we were prisoners.

The young Ladies were pleased, and so were some of our auditors, for by that time we had plenty at the door, hearing something they had never heard before, it had excited their curiosity. Evening came and brought with it its usual employment of walking, &c. &c. and no danger dreamt on.

The next morning, at seven o'clock, I was awakened by a most prodigious noise at my door, and some one on the outside bidding me get up instantly and open it. I at first thought I was dreaming, but I soon found by the incessant noise, that it was but too true. I told them if they would have a moment's patience, I would open it as soon as I had got some of my clothes on ; I did so ; when what should present itself to my astonished view, but five soldiers with their muskets and fixed bayonets, and the mayor at the head of them. "Come, Citizen, you must go with us to the district." I was rivetted to the spot, and almost lost the power of thought ; but they soon moved me, and they led me like a sheep to the slaughter, without resistance or complaint. When we got into the town, the freshness of the morning air a little recovered me: The mayor walked by my side, two men went before, and the other three behind ; as I found that the guard did not keep very close to us. I took an opportunity to ask the mayor (in a whisper) to tell me what it all meant. He replied in the same under-tone for fear of being heard by our guard, your countryman, Colonel Keating, has denounced you for singing "God save the King" *(Votre aire National.)* Good God! thought I, what shall I do ! (after a little re-

flection) it is no use I thought to suffer myself to
be cast down—I might die in a worse cause; and
so it must take its chance.

On entering the Hall of Audience I found all
the members of the district sitting with their President, at that early hour, at the head of a large
table covered over with a cloth, that had once
been green, the Secretary was sitting at the bottom of the table, with his pens, ink, and paper,
ready to take down the deposition against poor
me; the room was very lofty and wainscotted
half way up with dark oak, no doubt some hundred
years old, which cast a gloom over the place I
shall never forget: add to which, the grave faces
of my judges, gave it altogether a very dismal
appearance; and I thought that the guillotine
was already staring me in the face. I had time
for all these reflections and observations before
the President addressed me. At length, he spoke
as follows, in a solemn tone of voice: " Citizen,
we have been well informed, that you have offended against the Laws of the Republic; and
that you have set at defiance its just decrees and
ordinances, and that you have in despight thereof,
and contrary to the law of the land, which inflicts
the punishment of death, on all who shall speak,
or sing in favour of kings; and yet, Citizen, you

have dared to do this." " Now, what have you to plead in extenuation of the crime you have committed, and why the law should not be put in force against you? Speak. With a firm look and a firm voice I replied, " Citizen President, as I have your permission, I must in the first place state, that if I have offended against the laws of the Republic, it has been done in ignorance of any such decree, for what passes in the *great world* never penetrates the *walls of our prison.* In the next place, I am not a subject of this country, and therefore owe it no allegiance, and also that I am detained here as a prisoner, contrary to the Laws of Nations, and you might just as well order me not to speak my native language as to say, that I shall not sing the national air of my own country if I think proper. At the same time I would wish you to understand, that had I known that such a law had been passed, I might have been tempted not to *run* the *risk* of giving offence, but as I did not know it, I plead " Not guilty." And I shall only add, that we were singing for our amusement, without attaching any further consequence to it, or thought of giving offence to any one, much less to the Republic. They turned to each other and talked in a low voice for several minutes, when the President said, " Citizen, will you assure me that

M

you did not know of the law which forbids any one to speak in favour of kings, and that you were *only* singing your national air for *your* amusement?" I replied, " Citizen President, I do assure you on my word of honour that I had no other idea in so doing." " Very well," said the President, " then since that is the case, I do not think there is any occasion to detain you any longer." I thanked them, and assured them that nothing more was meant. The little secretary started up and said, " he had the pleasure of knowing me for a person that would not offend against the laws of the Republic on any account. The countenances of my judges relaxed of their severity, and they wished me a good morning. I returned the compliment, highly pleased that I had got off so well.

As I was leaving the hall, at the door of which stood the little friendly mayor, he took hold of my hand and shook it most cordially, saying, (with a face lit up with smiles of benignity and humanity) " *We have not forgot the garden adventure,* and beware of *bad neighbours.*" "Good morning! good morning!" said I, " and away I tripped as I came, with my *five footmen* before and behind, back to my cage.

(It may not be amiss to mention that it was private pique only that made Colonel Keating denounce me, because I would not speak to his kept mistress, as they lived in the very next room to mine; and according to his notions of *equality*, he *thought there* could be no *harm* in my doing so. This Colonel Keating quarrelled with his own government, sold his commission and his private property, and went to reside at Brussels. Soon after his going there, the Belgians revolted against the Emperor, and he coincided with them. He was also at the head of the Corresponding Society in London.

Mr. Pitt laid an embargo on a ship in the river, laden with arms for the rebels of Belgium, which was furnished to them by the disaffected in England of that day.) As soon as I reached *home*, burning with rage at the treacherous conduct of Colonel Keating, (which might have cost me my life, and no thanks *to him* that it did not) with both my hands I beat against his door; and to tell the truth, I do not think I called him a gentleman.

By that time it was near ten o'clock (and not having been in the habit of *walking* for *some months past so early in the town.)* I wished for my breakfast, but that pleasure was denied me, till I had answered five hundred questions to as many people (the whole prison was in an uproar) and Frenchman like, all talking at once, for they were dying with impatience to know what it all meant, but when I had told them, they declared they never heard any thing so barbarous or unmanly; and one and all declared that they never would speak or notice him more, or his fellow-companion the *Patriot* from Newcastle, so *they were*, what is commonly called, " sent to Coventry."

Just about this time the death of Robespierre, on the 9th of August, and other violent commotions took place in Paris, left us in doubt as to our own fate, not knowing under whose reign of terror we might fall next; but in a little time we were quiet for our fears, as things began to take a milder turn, and about the middle of September a great number of the nobility were permitted to return to their own homes, subject to a guard at their *doors;* but that was more for *appearance* sake than from any real *motive;* they were *afraid* of being too *lenient* at first, as that hydra-headed monster, the Jacobin party, was so recently put down.

A fresh disposition of the prisoners took place. The English, with some few others, were re-manded to our old lodgings *La Providence.* There I met with a fresh supply, collected from all the other prisons in the town, and a motley group they were, for many of them (poor souls!) had worn their clothes *too long* to be of much service to them: and those were chiefly English. Here again I met my husband, and that was the last prison we had; but they kept the English, by way of a *bon bouche,* till the last; and we did not get out till the 28th of November, 1794, near fifteen months' imprisonment, without a possibility of receiving one sixpenny piece from our own country, to soften the rigours of con-finement. The hardships which the English suffered, for want of money, is beyond descrip-tion.

CHAPTER XVII.

OUT OF PRISON.

AGAIN returned to our houses and homes, we were like so many birds that had been long shut up in a cage, and when the door was opened for them, they flew about not knowing where to settle, so it was with us. Society was broken up, and every one was afraid of speaking to his neighbour, for why he knew not, such was the dread on the spirits.

About Christmas I became acquainted with an English lady (a lady by birth) who with her husband resided in Ameins, but he being a Frenchman, she fortunately escaped the effects of the decree against the English. She was and is, (for I believe she is still living) a niece of the present earl of H—on. She was a most amiable and sensible woman, and deserving of a much better fate than the one she met with in a husband. We had many pleasant parties at her house, when, one day among the rest, André Dumont, the deputy, dined there; in the course of conversation, I took an opportunity of asking him how it happened that Colonel Keating, that *good patriot*, should have been the first of the English who was sent to prison, and the last liberated? He laid his hand on mine, and said, very emphatically, though we may like the treason, it does not follow that we should love the traitor. I thought those few words spoke volumes, and were worthy of being recorded.

My husband's health was in a very precarious state, and we wished much to come to England; but the communication between the two countries were as close as ever. The district could not grant us a passport: it could only be obtained (if it could be had at all) by personal application in Paris. The time of the year (January) rendered it impossible for my husband to go there. At last it was decided by the district, that they would send his signalement (personal description) by me, begging the district in Paris, to grant us a passport for the month of April following. This I took with me, as I had other

business to settle there, which I knew would take
me some time. I arranged my affairs in consequence, and having left my husband in the care
of some good friends, I set off by the Diligence
as soon as it was day (and a very cold one it was.)
We arrived in Paris half frozen to death ; it was
in that very cold winter 1795, just at the time
that the French took Holland.

CHAPTER XVIII.

DETAINED BY FOUR HUNDRED FISHWOMEN, MESDAMES DE LA HALLE.

WHEN I arrived in Paris the cold was so intense that very little business was doing, as no one would stir out that could help it. We were deprived almost of the three first necessaries of life—bread, water, and fire. To give some idea of the distress I shall only mention that I gave *three shillings* and *sixpence per pound* for bread, and that was brought from a place called Mudon, at the distance of thirty miles from Paris. Wood was dear in proportion; and the water could not be obtained without the greatest difficulty. It would be in vain to attempt to enumerate the thousands who died of cold and hunger that winter in Paris. Misery was at its height.

N

At length the vernal season came round, which liberated the waters and us. The misery of the people during the winter, had kept Paris in a state of disquietude. At length the people revolted against the Convention, who had bought up all the grain, which they delivered out in such quantity, and at such *price* as they thought proper. The war was going on in Holland, and great quantities of the grain was sent to the armies. The people were generally displeased with the government; and early in the month of April the two suburbs of St. Antoine and St. Marceau declared war againt the Convention, and marched against it with four pieces of cannon, and threatened to fire on them, unless their demands were answered. It seemed ordained by fate, that if any thing unpleasant was going on, I was sure to come in for my share of it—so it was that day.

I had occasion to go most mornings to the Louvre, (at that time not a great deal unlike our Somerset House, as all the offices under government were kept there.) I was not in the least aware of what was passing, till I got to the place *De Carousel*; Paris not being blessed with those noisy fellows called horns in the street, whose business it is to let every one know what is pass-

ing and sometimes what is not. The seeing an
assemblage of persons was then so common in
Paris, that without paying any attention to it, I
kept walking on till I was stopped by a body
of four hundred women of the lowest class,
all talking at once—I was laid hold of by
ten or a dozen of them, who said, " Come,
Citizen, come, you must join us, and assist in
demanding more corn, cheaper, and of a better
quality. Certainly that which was delivered out
to those poor people was bad enough. Resistance to their will would have been vain. I
therefore made a virtue of necessity, and com-
plied with as good a grace as I could; it was
then between ten and eleven, the sun darting hot
upon us; they detained me there for several
hours, and what with the fatigue of walking and
standing, the heat and the noise, I thought I
must have fainted; I had an idea of telling them
that I was an Englishwoman, and had nothing
to do with their quarrels; but prudence forbade
that, as I had heard them exclaiming against the
English, saying, " it was their fault that *they*
were without bread."

I saw several members of the Convention in
very great danger of being killed in endeavouring
to pacify the mob, but fortunately there was no

one hurt materially. During this time I had been making my observations on my *light troop;* and I found that some of the women had more influence than others, and that they had a sort of ringleaders amongst them (if I may be allowed the expression) so I addressed myself to one, (not the most placid,) and told her that if she would permit me, I thought I could be of service to them. " As how?" said she. " I told her I had a friend in the Victualling Office, and that if they would allow me to speak to him, that I could make him understand what they wanted better, than so many speaking at once.' " Aye; she thought so too; she would consider of it; she left me to consult her companions, when it was decided, that I should in the name of the whole body then assembled, make known to them at the Victualling Office their distresses and their wants, and praying for an alleviation of their misery. I promised them I would (and sorry enough I was that I had it not in my power to be as good as my word, for I knew no one,) but it was the only way left me to get out of their power.

I advanced towards the Louvre: there was a very strong guard at all the doors; my *Ladies* accompanied me a part of the way, when the

officer of the guard, who had kept his eye pretty
well upon what was passing amongst us, seeing a
woman advance alone, asked me where I was
going and what I wanted? (being out of hearing
of the women) I told him how I was circum-
stanced, and that I had been detained ever since
eleven o'clock in the morning by them, and
begged he would let me pass. He smiled and
said, " As you are not one of *them*, I will let
you through." He did so ; I entered the Louvre,
and went through it ; and after various turnings,
I found myself at the upper end of the *Rue St.
Honoré ;* but my troubles were not to end so
soon. I had heard a cannonading for some hours,
at intervals, but did not know in what direction.
Upon inquiring at a shop (for I saw no one in
the street near me) I was informed, that it was
on the quay, and sometimes along the street I
was then in, which fully accounted for its being
so deserted. I was scarcely answered when a
shot was fired, which struck the upper parts of
the houses, and shattered some windows (they
used grape shot.) I staid some little time in the
shop, not knowing how I should get home, and
had some conversation with the mistress of it.
She told me that they did not fire above once in
ten or a dozen minutes. I staid till another shot
was fired, and then thought I might venture on

my return home (which was directly in the very teeth of it) as I lived in the *Rue de Grenelle*, past the Palais Royal, and the shop I had entered was nearly facing the church of St. Roche. I ran a little, and then entered another shop, where I found others in the same predicament with myself. At last, with a great deal of fatigue and danger, I succeeded in gaining the Palais Royal, through which I passed, and got safe to my hotel. From a little after ten in the morning (and it was then near six in the evening) had I been on foot without any refreshment.

Many persons lost their lives that day, and the corner of the Louvre next the river, and many houses in the Rue St. Honoré, show the marks to this hour of that day's exploit. Such are the blessings of Revolutions.

All my efforts to obtain a passport for England, or any other country, proved ineffectual. The other business which I had in hand being nearly brought to a conclusion, in about a week after I left Paris, and returned home, much vexed at my bad success.

CHAPTER XIX.

RETURN TO AMIENS, AND FINAL RETURN TO ENGLAND.

ON my return home I found my husband apparently not much worse; the summer advancing, his complaint being that flattering disorder a decline, we lived in hopes of his recovery.

During my absence there had been a great number of British officers at Amiens on their way to England. Some were waiting there for passports on parole—some their exchange—among the latter, were two officers of the —— foot, with their exchange in their pockets; but they could not leave the town, being in debt some few pounds, and not having a shilling in their pockets to pay with, or to take them to the seaside. In this dilemma they made their case known to my husband, who commisserated the situation of his countrymen, and British officers, who had been fighting the enemies of their country. He thought that while he had a guinea in his pocket, such men were entitled to share it with him. He let them have fifteen pounds (all they wanted) and they gave him a note on their agents for the amount, but which was never paid.

The death of my husband did not take place till the end of April in the following year; and what made his death doubly painful to me was, that although in a country whose population had so lately imbrued their hands in the blood of their SOVEREIGN, and in the blood of so many *thousands* of *innocent* victims; yet, at *that time* made *pretensions* to *religion*, and would not suffer my husband to be buried in consecrated ground, because he was a *Protestant,* or in *their* words, a *Heretic;* and his remains lie buried in a common field without one memento to say, " Here lies *one,* who was once a Christian, and an Englishman."

It was not till a year after, that I had any chance of obtaining a passport, and for which I was obliged once more to go to Paris. Buonaparte was then gaining great popularity, and by degrees every thing was beginning to shew the presence of a master, and order was again rising from the bed of chaos.

General Buonaparte inspected the troops *en parade* every morning, where I frequently saw him. I could not help taking notice of a man who had made so considerable a noise in the world, even at that time. I scrutinized his person very much, but found nothing in it prepossessing: His countenance was rather sombre than otherwise, and every turn of his eye was marked with suspicion; and I thought while I contemplated it, that if the face is the index to the human mind, then gloom and mischief dwelt triumphant in his.

At last, with great difficulty, I obtained my passport, and came home by the way of Dunkirk, in the month of August, 1797.—I returned to dear England with a much greater love of my country than before I left it, and a much higher esteem for its laws and the administration of them.

In England no man ever need be afraid of being taken out of his bed at midnight, and sent no one knows where, or thrown into a dungeon, or guillotined, for no one knows what. Oh! may the Constitution of England, and her Laws in all their purity hold, as long as Albion's proud head shall stand above the level of the sea, or till time shall be no more; and may the heart of every true-born Briton join with me in the same sentiment, is my sincere wish.

And now permit me to take leave of my kind Readers, who have followed me through all my misfortunes and hair-breadth escapes; and let me conclude (I hope without impiety) nearly in the words of the Litany, " from Battle, Murder, *and* Revolutions, Good Lord deliver us !"

21 OC 62

FINIS.

Richards & Co. Printers, 3, Grocers' Hall Court, Ponltry.

CPSIA information can be obtained at www.ICGtesting.com

229202LV00003B/33-34/P

9 781241 597245